Holiday Feasts
Festive Cooking for Family and Friends

BY LOU SEIBERT PAPPAS
ILLUSTRATIONS BY CAROLYN VIBBERT

CHRONICLE BOOKS
SAN FRANCISCO

Acknowledgments

With many thanks to the friends who shared their holiday traditions:
Mary Tift, Judy Fucilla, Mary Fortney, Pat Robinson, Marilyn Duvivier,
Karin Schulz, and Phyllis Thompson. What a pleasure to work again
with Meesha Halm, a delightful, thorough copy editor.

Printed in Hong Kong.
Pappas, Lou Seibert.
    Holiday Feasts: festive cooking for family and friends / by Lou Seibert Pappas : illustrations by Carolyn Vibbert.
      p.   cm.
    ISBN 0-8118-0264-7
    I. Christmas cookery.   2. Thanksgiving cookery.   3. Menus
  I. Title.
  TX739.2.C45P35   1993
  641.5'68–dc20

Distributed in Canada by Raincoast Books, 112 East Third Ave., Vancouver, B.C. V5T 1C8

10 9 8 7 6 5 4 3 2 1

Chronicle Books
275 Fifth Street
San Francisco, CA 94103

Table of Contents

A Thanksgiving Family Feast
with All the Trimmings   11

Holiday Open House after Caroling   25

Trim a Tree Supper   33

A Christmas Eve Fête   39

Christmas Morning Brunch   51

A Festive Christmas Dinner   61

Food Gifts   69

Index   72

THE HOLIDAY SEASON FROM THANKSGIVING TO CHRISTMAS IS A TIME OF NOSTALGIA AND FOR CELEBRATING AGAIN THE FOOD TRADITIONS SAVORED OVER THE YEARS. GIVING, SHARING, AND FEASTING PREVAIL.

A SPIRITUAL DELIGHT UNFOLDS IN RECREATING THE BELOVED DISHES AND MENUS OF HAPPY TIMES PAST WHEN THE FAMILY AND FRIENDS GATHERED AROUND THE TABLE. SENTIMENTAL FEELINGS ARE IGNITED AS CHERISHED AROMAS WAFT THE AIR AND A LADEN BUFFET HOLDS PRIZE DISHES THAT REAPPEAR JUST FOR THESE FESTIVITIES. AS THE YEARS PASS, AND NEW GENERATIONS CREATE THEIR OWN CUSTOMS AND START THEIR OWN FAMILIES, HOLDING ON TO THE LEGENDARY DISHES BECOMES MORE MEANINGFUL AND MEMORABLE.

THANKSGIVING LAUNCHES THE HOLIDAY SEASON WITH A TRADITIONAL FAMILY FEAST CENTERING AROUND NATIVE FOODS THAT THE PILGRIMS AND INDIANS SHARED THREE CENTURIES AGO. IN 1621, THE NEW SETTLERS OF MASSACHUSETTS STAGED A HARVEST FESTIVAL TO CELEBRATE THEIR SURVIVAL THROUGH THE FIRST HARD WINTER, THANKFUL FOR THE FRUITS OF THEIR HARVEST AND PEACE WITH THEIR INDIAN NEIGHBORS.

THEIR INDIAN FRIENDS, SQUANTO AND CHIEF MASSASOIT, SHOWED UP WITH 90 BRAVES AND THE EATING AND DRINKING WENT ON FOR THREE DAYS. THEY CONSUMED WILD DUCK, GOOSE, VENISON, LOBSTERS, OYSTERS, EELS, LEEKS, WATERCRESS, CRANBERRIES, WHEAT AND CORN BREADS, WILD PLUMS, AND DRIED BERRIES AND QUAFFED HOMEMADE WINE AND ALE.

ALTHOUGH WILD TURKEY WAS PLENTIFUL, THERE IS NO RECORD THAT IT WAS SERVED ON THAT FIRST THANKSGIVING. IT WAS NOT LISTED IN A MENU DRAWN UP BY WILLIAM BRADFORD, THEN GOVERNOR OF THE PLYMOUTH COLONY. FROM THIS BEGINNING, THANKSGIVING OCCURRED IRREGULARLY — THE DATE VARIED AND YEARS WERE SKIPPED. THE FIRST NATIONAL PROCLAMATION WAS ISSUED BY GEORGE WASHINGTON IN 1789, THE YEAR OF HIS INAUGURATION. IN 1863, PRESIDENT ABRAHAM LINCOLN PROCLAIMED THE LAST THURSDAY OF NOVEMBER AS A NATIONAL HOLIDAY, A DAY OF THANKSGIVING. SINCE THEN EACH PRESIDENT HAS CONTINUED THE PATTERN.

TODAY THE BIG BIRD — TURKEY — REIGNS SUPREME, AUGMENTED BY SUCH INDIGENOUS ESSENTIALS AS CRANBERRIES, PUMPKIN, NUTS, AND APPLES PLUS OTHER SIDE DISHES FOR A BOUNTIFUL, SOUL-SATISFYING

DINNER WITH ALL THE TRIMMINGS, YET REFLECTIVE OF A COUNTRY TABLE. SOME SAY THE BASIC MENU ELICITS A YEARNING FOR THE "FOLK" LIFE.

TODAY'S CELEBRATION OF THANKSGIVING IS OFTEN A COOPERATIVE ONE WITH SEVERAL GENERATIONS OR FAMILIES SHARING IN THE SPREAD. EVERY FAMILY DRAWS ON ITS HERITAGE, OFTEN STYLING A MENU WITH A CROSS-CULTURAL DIVERSITY REFLECTING ITS ECLECTIC BACKGROUND. THIS DAY USHERS IN THE UPCOMING HOLIDAYS.

HRISTMAS IS A MAGICAL SEASON FOR CHILDREN AND A BUSY WHIRLWIND ONE FOR ADULTS. IT OFFERS AN OCCASION FOR SEEING OLD FRIENDS AND MEETING NEW ONES. GIFT GIVING AND FEASTING TAKE PRECEDENCE, YET OVER THE YEARS, IT IS THE FOODS OF CHRISTMAS THAT FORM A LEITMOTIF THAT IS EVERLASTING.

THE ROOTS OF OUR AMERICAN CHRISTMAS ARE MANIFOLD WITH CUSTOMS DRAWN FROM THE IMMIGRANTS FROM MANY LANDS. AS EARLY AS THE FOURTH CENTURY A.D., CHRISTIANS ADOPTED DECEMBER 25TH AS CHRIST'S BIRTHDAY AND SET ASIDE EPIPHANY — THE TWELFTH DAY OF CHRISTMAS — FOR THE ARRIVAL OF THE WISE MEN AND FOR CHRIST'S BAPTISM. EARLY FESTIVITIES WOVE INTO THE BIBLICAL TALE ASPECTS OF

PAGAN CELEBRATIONS OF THE WINTER SOLSTICE AND THE WEEK-LONG ROMAN SATURNALIA.

IN AMERICA, FEELINGS TOWARD CHRISTMAS WERE DIVIDED ACCORDING TO RELIGIOUS DENOMINATION. CHRISTMAS WAS BANNED BY THE STERN PURITAN ANCESTORS AND THEY REACTED STRONGLY TO ANYTHING THAT REMINDED THEM OF "RELICS OF POPERY." SINCE THE MAJORITY OF THE EARLIEST SETTLERS WERE PROTESTANTS, HAILING FROM ENGLAND OR GERMANY, FOR A TIME THE PURITAN ETHIC PREVAILED. THE ANTAGONISM BETWEEN THE CATHOLIC AND PROTESTANT FAITHS AND OTHER SECTS LASTED UNTIL ABOUT 1750. THE DIMINISHING OBJECTION TO CELEBRATING THE HOLIDAY WAS HASTENED BY THE RAPID GROWTH OF THE COUNTRY AS A WHOLE AND THE INTERMINGLING OF PERSONS OF DIFFERENT NATIONAL AND RELIGIOUS BACKGROUNDS. ALABAMA WAS THE FIRST STATE TO GRANT LEGAL RECOGNITION TO CHRISTMAS IN 1836 AND BY 1890 ALL STATES AND TERRITORIES HAD MADE SIMILAR ACKNOWLEDGMENTS.

SINCE THE MIDDLE AGES, THE YULE LOG AND EVERGREENS, SYMBOLIZING SURVIVAL AND ETERNAL LIFE, HAVE BEEN ASSOCIATED WITH THE SEASON. FROM THE GERMANS, AMERICANS ADOPTED THE PRACTICE OF

CUTTING AND DECORATING A TREE, AND SUNDAY SCHOOL DID MUCH TO PROMOTE THE ACCEPTANCE OF THE CHRISTMAS TREE AND SANTA CLAUS.

THE FAMOUS DICTUM, MERRY CHRISTMAS AND HAPPY NEW YEAR, WAS COINED BY BRITON THOMAS COLE IN 1843 WHEN HE CREATED THE FIRST CHRISTMAS CARD, WHICH DEPICTED A FAMILY CELEBRATION. WITHIN A FEW YEARS GREETING CARDS BECAME VERY POPULAR IN ENGLAND. IN BOSTON IN 1874, LITHOGRAPHER LOUIS PRANGE PRODUCED THE FIRST GREETING CARDS FOR SALE IN AMERICA, AND BY THE 1890S CARD SENDING WAS A RITUAL IN THIS COUNTRY. THE MAJORITY OF OUR MOST REVERED CHRISTMAS CAROLS ALSO DATE FROM THE 19TH CENTURY.

ALTHOUGH CHRISTMAS HAS ITS ORIGIN IN A HOLY DAY, THE SECULAR ASPECTS OF THE HOLIDAY HAVE BECOME IMPORTANT WITH GIFT GIVING AND FEASTING, AS WELL AS SHARING TOYS AND FOOD FOR THE NEEDY.

GATHERINGS SUCH AS CAROLING, WHICH HAD ORIGINATED IN THE 13TH CENTURY IN ENGLAND, CHURCH SING-ALONGS, AND SUPPERS FOLLOWING THE CHRISTMAS PAGEANT ARE ALL SEASONAL PLEASURES FOR REINFORCING FRIENDSHIPS. TREE TRIMMING, COOKIE EXCHANGES, OPEN HOUSES, AND FIRESIDE SOUP SUPPERS ARE OTHER OCCASIONS FOR HAPPY TIMES AND ENJOYING A REPAST TOGETHER.

An open house soup supper with family and friends provides a festive dining event that is easy on the hostess and a pleasure for the guests. For a tree—trimming party, pasta makes a stylish, speedy entree, and for a fête on Christmas Eve, seafood is ever popular.

For the Christmas Day dinner, family custom dictates the entree, be it wild duck, turkey, ham, or beef. An English favorite is standing rib roast with Yorkshire pudding and such classic accompaniments as smoked salmon and steamed pudding or a yule log for dessert.

Throughout the season, there is a return to the time-honored task of baking holiday breads ahead and filling tins with cookies and candies so they are ready to pass around for impromptu gatherings or parties. Most individuals like a varied selection of delicious morsels from around the world to round out the holiday table.

Treasured dishes that reappear year after year set the stage for future heart-warming celebrations, and it becomes a family custom to pass along these revered recipes from generation to generation.

A Thanksgiving Family Feast with All the Trimmings

VINTNER'S BROTH WITH SHERRY (OPTIONAL)

RELISH PLATTER:
NIÇOISE OLIVES, ROQUEFORT-STUFFED FENNEL, DILLED GREEN BEANS,
SHRIMP-STUFFED CHERRY TOMATOES

GREEN SALAD WITH AVOCADO, PINK GRAPEFRUIT, AND POMEGRANATE SEEDS

ROAST TURKEY WITH SAGE STUFFING

CRANBERRY APPLE RELISH

ROASTED YAMS   CARAMELIZED SWEET ONIONS

GLAZED CARROTS   GREEN BEANS WITH HERBS

PRALINE PECAN PUMPKIN PIE   CINNAMON CRISP APPLE PIE

SAUVIGNON BLANC OR GAMAY BEAUJOLAIS

TRADITION REIGNS ON THIS ALL-AMERICAN HOLIDAY WITH CLASSICS DRAWN FROM OUR FOREBEARERS. What's important is creating an ongoing repetition of the soul-satisfying dishes once savored at mother's table.

An enticing starter is a pass-around soup as simple as consomme laced with sherry and served in Chinese teacups or small mugs. For a chic relish platter, assemble Niçoise olives, fennel sticks stuffed with Roquefort, pickled green beans in dill, and cherry tomatoes, split and stuffed with shrimp.

The big bird is the regal focal point with its homespun celery-studded stuffing and tangy cranberry relish. A piquant grapefruit and avocado salad and a quartet of vegetables augment the table. A Sauvignon Blanc or Gamay Beaujolais will please aficionados of white or red wine. On the dessert sideboard, toasted pecans seal a pumpkin pie and a cinnamon streusel cloaks an apple pie for a gala finale to this grand feast.

Green Salad with Avocado, Pink Grapefruit, and Pomegranate Seeds

This salad is an eye-catcher: a pinwheel of pink grapefruit and avocado, showered with pomegranate seeds, tops the salad greens.

Lemon-Tarragon Dressing:
¼ cup olive oil
¼ cup canola oil
3 tablespoons lemon juice
1 teaspoon grated lemon zest
½ teaspoon crumbled dried tarragon
2 teaspoons Dijon mustard
Salt and freshly ground pepper to taste

2 pink grapefruit
2 large avocados
Juice of ½ lemon
1 head each butter lettuce
  and red leaf lettuce
½ cup pomegranate seeds

PREPARE THE LEMON-TARRAGON DRESSING: In a small bowl, whisk together the oils, lemon juice and zest, tarragon, mustard, salt, and pepper until blended.

PEEL AND SECTION GRAPEFRUITS. Peel and slice avocados and sprinkle slices with lemon juice to prevent from darkening. Tear greens into bite-size pieces and place in a salad bowl. Pour over two-thirds of the dressing and toss to coat. Arrange grapefruit sections and avocado slices alternately on top. Sprinkle with pomegranate seeds. Drizzle with remaining dressing.

MAKES 8 SERVINGS.

Roast Turkey with Sage Stuffing

Thanksgiving dinner revolves around a beautifully browned, big, and succulent roast turkey. It may be classically stuffed or the dressing may be baked in a casserole alongside. Though our forebearers may not have savored turkey at their first Thanksgiving feast, it has become de rigueur, and most families glory in an annual preparation of time-honored accompaniments. The old-fashioned bread, celery, and onion stuffing with sage remains a prime favorite, although every family interjects its own ingredients.

20 pound turkey

Salt and pepper to taste

$\frac{1}{3}$ cup lemon juice

$1\frac{1}{4}$ cups butter

2 large onions, finely chopped

1 small inner head celery, finely chopped

2 tablepoons minced fresh sage or 2 teaspoons
  crumbled dried sage

1 tablespoon minced fresh thyme or 1 teaspoon
  crumbled dried thyme

Salt and freshly ground black pepper to taste

2 loaves sweet or sourdough French bread,
  torn into cubes and air-dried 1 day (about
  10 cups croutons)

$\frac{1}{4}$ cup chopped parsley

1 to $1\frac{1}{2}$ cups turkey or chicken stock
  (approximately)

1 cup diced dried apricots (optional)

1 cup golden raisins (optional)

REMOVE NECK, GIZZARD, AND OTHER INNARDS FOUND INSIDE THE CARCASS. Wash thoroughly. To prepare turkey stock, place neck and innards in a saucepan and cover with water. Add salt and pepper to taste. Cover and simmer 2 hours; strain and reserve stock. Or substitute prepared chicken stock.

WASH TURKEY INSIDE AND OUT AND PAT DRY. Rub the entire surface as well as the cavity with lemon juice and sprinkle with salt and pepper. In a large skillet, melt 1 cup butter over medium high heat and saute onions and celery until glazed. Season with sage, thyme, salt, and pepper. Place bread in a bowl, add sauteed vegetables, parsley, and enough stock to barely moisten lightly. If desired, mix in apricots and raisins. Stuff inside the turkey, filling three-fourths full as the stuffing will expand. Close the openings with small skewers and a criss-crossed string. Or if desired, place stuffing in a greased 3 quart casserole. Place turkey on a rack in a roasting pan, breast side up, and insert a meat thermometer between the thigh and the body of the bird, taking care that it is not in contact with the bone. Pour 1 cup of water into the bottom of pan. Melt remaining $\frac{1}{4}$ cup butter with $\frac{1}{4}$ cup water and brush the turkey with it. With a brush, baste the turkey with the juices in the pan every 20 to 30 minutes during roasting. Roast in a preheated 325 degree oven until a meat thermometer registers 170 degrees, about 3 to 3$\frac{1}{2}$ hours. Transfer to a board. Carefully spoon out all of the stuffing into a serving dish. Let the turkey rest for 15 to 20 minutes before carving.

MAKES ABOUT 16 SERVINGS.

NOTE: Some cooks prefer to roast the turkey breast down during the first 1$\frac{1}{2}$ hours. To do this, place it on a rack covered with heavily greased parchment, foil, or brown paper to keep the skin from tearing when turning the turkey. Then turn it breast-side up for the balance of the roasting. This method creates moister white meat.

It is important to stuff the turkey just before roasting, not in advance. Once baked, remove it from the bird immediately and refrigerate any leftovers swiftly.

Cranberry Apple Relish

This three-fruit relish is a bright, zesty accompaniment to the bird. For those who like a lively flavor zip, incorporate the ginger

2 oranges

3 large tart apples, quartered and cored

1 pound whole cranberries

½ cup sugar

3 tablespoons golden raisins (optional)

WITH A VEGETABLE PEELER, PEEL ZEST FROM THE ORANGES; SET ASIDE. Peel off and discard the white pith and cut oranges into eighths. Place half of the oranges, orange zest, apples, cranberries, and sugar in a food processor fitted with a steel blade. Process until finely chopped. Turn out mixture into a container. Put the remaining ingredients in the food processor and process until finely chopped. Add to the other cranberry mixture and mix to combine. Cover and refrigerate for several hours before serving. Keeps refrigerated for 2 to 3 days.

GINGER VARIATION: Peel and chop 1 tablespoon fresh ginger and process with the other ingredients.

Cranberries freeze beautifully. Simply slip a package in a plastic bag, tie, and freeze for later pleasure.

MAKES ABOUT 1 3/4 QUARTS.

The American Indians invented cranberry sauce, sweetening the berries with maple sugar or honey. They ate the berries raw as well as cooked and pounded them with dried meat and melted animal fat to produce pemmican. Cranberries were one of the first native American fruits to be shipped to Europe commercially.

Roasted Yams

In America, the word yam has often been used as a synonym for the sweet potato, yet they are botanically different and the yam has more natural sugar and a moister texture.

6 to 8 medium yams or sweet potatoes
Butter

Salt and freshly ground pepper to taste

PRICK THE SKIN OF THE YAMS IN SEVERAL PLACES. Place in a baking pan and roast in a preheated 375 to 400 degree oven for 1 to 1¼ hours or until tender. Halve and serve with butter, salt, and pepper.

MAKES 8 TO 10 SERVINGS.

Glazed Carrots

Caramelized brown sugar with Dijon mustard creates a lively lift for carrots. The combination comes from a dear artist friend, now in her eighties, whose food etchings adorn my walls.

6 to 8 large carrots, peeled and sliced on the diagonal
2 tablespoons butter
1 tablespoon Dijon mustard

1 tablespoon firmly packed brown sugar
Salt and freshly ground pepper to taste

In a saucepan, cook carrots in a small amount of boiling salted water until tender, about 6 to 8 minutes; drain well. Add the butter, mustard, sugar, salt, and pepper and stir gently to coat. Cook over medium heat until carrots are glazed.

MAKES 8 SERVINGS.

Caramelized Sweet Onions

With oven roasting, sweet onions develop caramelized juices that are succulent when deglazed with wine vinegar and reabsorbed into their soft interior.

6 to 8 Walla Walla, Vidalia, or other sweet onions,
*   about 3-inches in diameter, unpeeled*
Olive oil

Salt and freshly ground pepper to taste
¼ cup red wine vinegar
2 tablespoons balsamic vinegar

LEAVE ONIONS UNPEELED AND RUB SURFACES WITH OIL. Place onions on a baking pan. Sprinkle with salt and pepper. Bake in the middle of a preheated 375 degree oven for 45 minutes to 1 hour or until tender. Transfer onions to a platter. Halve onions horizontally leaving skin in place. Deglaze pan juices with vinegars by placing pan on top of the range and heating and scraping well with a wooden spoon. Let juices reduce and brush sauce over the open surfaces of the onions.

MAKES 8 SERVINGS.

"The onion is the truffle of the poor," wrote French gourmet Robert J. Courtine.

In 1624, Pierre Marquette told of being saved from starvation by eating nodding onions and tree onions, two native wild American varieties, when his explorations took him to the southern shore of Lake Michigan, later named Chicago, which commemorates its abundance in onions with the Indian word for their odor. (Waverley Root in "Food")

Green Beans with Herbs

A shower of herbs enhances slender green beans for a vegetable dish with wide appeal.

2 pounds slender green beans

2 tablespoons olive oil

3 tablespoons minced parsley

1 clove garlic, minced

1½ teaspoons chopped fresh tarragon or

½ teaspoon crumbled dried tarragon

TRIM ENDS FROM BEANS. If the beans are slender and small, leave whole; if not, cut in half lengthwise. Cook beans in a large pot of boiling salted water until crisp tender, about 5 to 7 minutes; drain. Add oil, parsley, garlic, and tarragon and heat, shaking pan to coat beans.

MAKES 8 SERVINGS.

Praline Pecan Pumpkin Pie

Pumpkin Pie is as integral to Thanksgiving as the big bird itself, yet over the years as the excellent winter squashes have filled the produce and farmers markets, good cooks have discovered that butternut or banana squash makes superior pie replacing the usual canned pumpkin. Lately, a new hybrid of pale, cream-colored pumpkin from Phipps Ranch in Pescadero provides fine-grained, flavorful orange pulp to fill this spicy pie. So good was the taste of this variety last year, that it is now growing in my garden. A caramelized nut topping makes a crunchy finish for this pumpkin pie.

Pastry Shell:

1 ¼ cups flour

¼ teaspoon salt

6 tablespoons butter

3 to 4 tablespoons ice water

3 eggs

¾ cup firmly packed brown sugar

½ teaspoon ground cinnamon

½ teaspoon ground ginger

¼ teaspoon ground cloves

¼ teaspoon ground nutmeg

½ teaspoon salt

1 ⅔ cups pureed cooked pumpkin, butternut,
    or banana squash

1 ¼ cups half-and-half or milk

¼ cup dark rum

Praline Pecan Topping:

¼ cup firmly packed brown sugar

⅔ cup pecan halves or walnut halves

Whipped cream for topping (optional)

PREPARE PASTRY SHELL: In a medium bowl or the bowl of a food processor, place the flour, salt, and butter, cut in ½ inch pieces. By hand, mix with a pastry blender or two knives, or process with the food processor until the consistency of coarse crumbs. Add water and mix until dough clings together. Pat dough into a ball, wrap in plastic wrap, and refrigerate for 20 minutes. Roll out dough on a lightly floured board to fit a 9-inch pie dish. Arrange in pie dish and flute edges. Place in the freezer for 15 minutes to firm up. Prick the bottom with a fork, then press a piece of heavy-duty foil into the pie shell.

Bake in the middle of a preheated 425 degree oven for 6 minutes; remove foil and bake for 4 minutes longer until just beginning to brown. Remove from oven and set aside.

IN A LARGE BOWL, BEAT EGGS UNTIL BLENDED. Mix in sugar, cinnamon, ginger, cloves, nutmeg, and salt. Stir in pumpkin or squash, half-and-half or milk, and rum. Pour into pre-baked pastry shell. Bake in the middle of a preheated 375 degree oven for 40 minutes or until set. Transfer to a cooling rack.

Just before serving, finish with Praline Pecan Topping: press brown sugar through a sieve over top of pie. Sprinkle with nuts. Broil until sugar melts and caramelizes, about 1 minute. Let cool on a rack. Serve warm or at room temperature. Top with whipped cream, if desired.

MAKES 6 TO 8 SERVINGS.

NOTE: If preferred, omit rum and replace it with ¼ cup milk and 1 teaspoon vanilla extract.

No mention is made of pumpkin being part of the first Thanksgiving, yet the Indians did raise some and served them boiled, roasted in ashes, baked with honey, or dried. The Pilgrims stewed "Pompion" and mixed it with Indian cornmeal to make bread. They also filled the pumpkin shell with milk, sugar, and spices and baked it in the fireplace.

A hand-written cookbook of Martha Washington relates how she laced her pumpkin pie filling "with a gill of brandy," a quarter of a nutmeg, and 1 tablespoon of ginger.

Pumpkins and squashes are uniquely American and were completely unknown to the Old World before the time of Columbus. It is possible that squash was the very first food to be cultivated by American Indians — first within what has been called the Indian triad of maize, beans, and squash, which constituted the basis of the Indian diet in both Americas.

Cinnamon Crisp Apple Pie

Apple is prized as the most popular American pie flavor. In this open-face version, a cinnamon streusel cloaks the sliced fruit.

Butter Pastry Shell:
1 cup unbleached or all-purpose flour
½ cup butter
2 tablespoons powdered sugar

7 large Granny Smith, Pippin, or
  Golden Delicious apples
1 tablespoon butter
2 tablespoons sugar
2 teaspoons grated lemon zest
3 tablespoons firmly packed brown sugar
1 teaspoon ground cinnamon
Whipped cream or vanilla ice cream
(optional)

PREPARE BUTTER PASTRY SHELL: In a bowl, place flour, butter, and powdered sugar. Mix until texture forms coarse crumbs; reserve 3 tablespoons for topping. Turn out remainder into a 10-inch pie pan or a 10-inch fluted flan pan with removable bottom. With fingertips press crumbs against sides of pan and with the heel of the palm press firmly against the bottom of pan. Place in the freezer for 10 minutes to firm up. Bake in the middle of a preheated 425 degree oven for 6 to 8 minutes or until barely browned on the edges. Remove from oven and place on a cooling rack.

PEEL, CORE, AND SLICE APPLES. In a large frying pan, melt butter over medium high heat, add sugar, apples, and lemon zest and cook, stirring, until apples are almost tender. Spoon into the baked pastry shell. Mix together the reserved 3 tablespoons of pastry crumbs, brown sugar, and cinnamon and sprinkle over the apples. Bake in the middle of a preheated 375 degree oven for 30 to 35 minutes or until apples are tender and top is lightly browned. Let cool to room temperature. If desired, serve with whipped cream or vanilla ice cream.

MAKES 8 SERVINGS.

Holiday Open House after Caroling

BLACK BEAN SOUP

SOUTHWEST SALAD

CRUSTY SOURDOUGH BREAD OR ROLLS

CHOCOLATE ALMOND TORTE

MULLED WINE

A WARMING SOUP SUPPER MAKES A GLORIOUS FINALE TO A CAROLING PARTY ON A FROSTY EVE. It is also ideal for a holiday open house with its easy-to-serve format. Greet guests with spiced wine and arrange a help-yourself buffet with a steaming pot of soup, a colorful salad, crusty rolls, and a regal chocolate torte.

Black Bean Soup

The beloved first grade teacher of our eldest commenced a custom of inviting friends and neighbors for soup on the two days preceding Christmas Eve. For 10 years, she and her two sons greeted up to 180 guests annually as the families trooped into her kitchen to ladle up a choice of hearty potages from a trio of bubbling cauldrons. A favorite moment came when the high school Madrigal singers would arrive and sing for their supper.

Bean, lentil, corn chowder, and turkey mulligatawny were favorites. Crusty loaves of sourdough from a coastside bakery accompanied them, and friends often contributed a bottle of wine, a chunk of cheese, or some cookies for embellishment. Going for Christmas soup became a cherished tradition for all ages.

Black beans create a hearty full-meal soup, ideal for a crowd.

2 pounds dried black beans	1 teaspoon ground allspice
Water	1 small dried red pepper, seeds removed and minced
1 ham shank, about 2 pounds	¼ cup red wine vinegar
2 medium-sized onions, medium chopped	2 cans (8 oz. each) tomato sauce
2 stalks celery or fennel with leaves, medium chopped	½ cup dry sherry (optional)
2 carrots, medium chopped	Salt and freshly ground black pepper to taste
4 cloves garlic, minced	Yogurt or sour cream and chopped cilantro or
1 bay leaf	parsley for garnish
2 teaspoons crumbled dried oregano	Lime wedges for garnish

PLACE THE BEANS IN A LARGE KETTLE. Add enough hot water to cover beans by 2 inches. Cover, bring to a boil, and boil for 2 minutes. Turn off the heat and let the beans soak, covered, for 1 hour; drain. Add 2½ quarts water to the beans, along with the ham shank, onion, celery, carrot, garlic, bay leaf, oregano, allspice, and pepper. Cover and simmer 1½ hours or until beans are almost tender. Add wine vinegar and tomato sauce and simmer until beans are tender, about 30 minutes longer. Discard bay leaf. Remove ham shank and chop it, discarding bones. Spoon about one-third of the beans and some liquid into a blender or food processor and process until smooth. Return the puree to the soup and add the sherry, if desired, and ham. Season with salt and pepper. If desired, refrigerate. To serve, heat through and ladle into bowls. Top each serving with a dollop of yogurt and sprinkle with cilantro or parsley. Garnish with lime wedges.

MAKES ABOUT 16 SERVINGS.

Southwest Salad

This colorful salad has a bright, inviting look and stands up well on a buffet table.

1 small head romaine

2 navel oranges, peeled and sliced very thinly

1 small cucumber, peeled and sliced thinly

1 small sweet red onion, sliced thinly and separated
   into rings

1 cup peeled, thinly sliced jicama

1 small red pepper, halved, seeded, and sliced
   thinly or diced

Citrus Dressing:

¼ cup olive oil

¼ cup orange juice

1 tablespoon lemon juice

1 teaspoon grated lemon zest

Salt and freshly ground pepper to taste

½ teaspoon crumbled dried oregano

TEAR ROMAINE INTO BITE-SIZE PIECES AND PLACE IN A SALAD BOWL. Arrange the orange, cucumber, onion, jicama, and pepper on top of the romaine.

PREPARE CITRUS DRESSING: In a small bowl, whisk together the oil, orange juice, lemon juice, lemon zest, salt, pepper, and oregano and pour dressing over salad. Toss lightly.

MAKES 6 TO 8 SERVINGS.

Chocolate Almond Torte

A chocolate cake is everyone's love and this one is seductive — intensely rich, yet light and crumbly, and wonderfully moist. When I was dining in a two-star restaurant in Burgundy with an entourage of American food editors one December, this gateau was the spectacular finale flanked by scoops of caramel and vanilla bean ice cream. The young chef came into the dining room and when prodded, related the formula in metric equations, enough for eight cakes. Back in the States, I eagerly recreated and refined the recipe and it has become my quintessential party torte ever since.

½ cup unsalted butter

8 ounces semisweet chocolate

5 eggs, separated

⅛ teaspoon salt

⅛ teaspoon cream of tartar

¾ cup sugar

2 tablespoons Grand Marnier or other
   orange-flavored liqueur

¾ cup finely ground almonds, toasted

6 tablespoons all-purpose flour

Chocolate Glaze:

1 ounce unsweetened chocolate

3 ounces semisweet chocolate

3 tablespoons unsalted butter

GREASE A 9-INCH SPRING-FORM PAN, and line with parchment; then rub paper with butter and lightly flour. In the top of a double boiler, melt butter and chocolate, stirring to blend. Let cool. In a large mixing bowl, beat egg whites until foamy, add salt and cream of tartar, and beat until soft peaks form. Add 3 tablespoons of the sugar and beat until stiff, glossy peaks form. In another bowl, beat egg yolks until thick and lemon-colored and beat in remaining sugar and liqueur. Stir in chocolate mixture. Fold in one-third of the whites to lighten the mixture. Then gently fold in the nuts, flour, and the remaining whites. Pour batter into parchment-lined pan and smooth out the top. Bake in the middle of a preheated 375 degree oven for 35 to 40 minutes or until the cake is set around the sides and the center four inches are still soft. Let cake cool on a rack. Place a serving plate on top of the cake pan and invert. Remove pan sides and carefully peel off parchment paper.

PREPARE CHOCOLATE GLAZE: Combine in the top of a double boiler the unsweetened and semisweet chocolate and butter. Melt over simmering water and stir until blended. Cool over ice for about 1 minute, until chocolate just begins to thicken. Pour glaze onto the cake and quickly spread with a spatula so glaze covers the top surface and coats the sides of cake.

MAKES 8 TO 10 SERVINGS.

Mulled Wine

Cozy and aromatic with spices and citrus, this is a cordial beverage for guests after a nippy eve of caroling or a day of skiing or skating. A jigger of brandy or cognac can lace the brew.

1 stick cinnamon, about 2 inches long
½ teaspoon whole cloves
Approximately ⅛ of a whole nutmeg
Juice of 1 lemon
Juice and thinly peeled zest of 1 orange
¼ cup firmly packed brown sugar
2 bottles (750 ml each) dry red wine
Orange slices for garnish

BREAK CINNAMON STICK INTO PIECES. Grind the cloves and nutmeg in a nutmeg grinder or coffee grinder. Place spices in a pot with lemon juice, orange juice and zest, brown sugar, and wine. Gently heat over low heat without boiling. Ladle into mugs and float a slice of orange on top.

NOTE: Use a knife to cut off a piece of a whole nutmeg. If desired, add a jigger of brandy or cognac.

MAKES 12 SERVINGS.

Trim a Tree Supper

TOASTED WALNUT, ENDIVE, AND APPLE SALAD

ANGEL HAIR PASTA WITH GINGER PRAWNS

STEAMED WHOLE ARTICHOKES

MOCHA MARRON COUPE

SAUVIGNON BLANC OR CHARDONNAY

FOR AN INFORMAL FAMILY SUPPER, when tree trimming takes priority, pasta with seafood is a welcome quick dish to prepare. Partner it with a sprightly endive salad and a glorious hot fudge sundae nuggeted with candied chestnuts splashed with cognac. This menu also makes a splendid repast for guests bid to an impromptu dinner.

Toasted Walnut, Endive, and Apple Salad

With red and green endive now growing in California and marketed across the country, it is appropriate to incorporate these delicacies in a holiday salad. Here they excel, balanced by the sweet overtones of apple and the toasty crunch of walnuts. Arugula is a taste-tingling addition with its peppery bite. It's handy in the kitchen garden as it is such an easy green to grow.

1 bunch arugula or watercress, stems removed

2 bunches red and green Belgian endive, separated
   into leaves and sliced into $\frac{1}{2}$-inch pieces

1 small head butter lettuce, torn into bite-size pieces

1 large Granny Smith or Fuji apple, halved, cored,
   and diced

Cassis Dressing:

2 tablespoons olive oil

2 tablespoons safflower oil

$1\frac{1}{2}$ tablespoons red wine vinegar

1 teaspoon cassis syrup

1 teaspoon Dijon mustard

1 shallot, chopped

Salt and freshly ground black pepper to taste

$\frac{1}{4}$ cup toasted walnut pieces

PLACE IN A SALAD BOWL the arugula, endive, lettuce, and apple.

PREPARE CASSIS DRESSING: In a small bowl, whisk together the oils, vinegar, cassis, mustard, shallot, salt, and pepper. Pour over greens and toss lightly. Spoon onto salad plates and scatter the nuts on top.

MAKES 4 SERVINGS.

NOTE: To lighten the dressing, add $1\frac{1}{2}$ tablespoons dry white wine.

Angel Hair Pasta with Ginger Prawns

Pasta is a winning favorite and this is an easy, elegant dish. The fresh tri-color angel hair pasta that comes in holiday colors of red, green, and white makes a handsome creation. Hot steamed artichokes are an ideal accompaniment.

1 cup clam juice, fish stock, or
    chicken stock

1 pound medium prawns (40 to
    a pound)

2 tablespoons olive oil

2 shallots, minced

3 cloves garlic, minced

2 teaspoons minced fresh ginger

2 teaspoons grated lemon zest

¾ cup dry white vermouth or dry
    white wine

1 tablespoon butter

12 ounces fresh angel hair pasta or
    8 ounces dried pasta

3 tablespoons chopped Italian parsley

¼ cup roasted pistachios, coarsely
    chopped

IN A SAUCEPAN, boil clam juice or stock until reduced to about ⅓ cup. Shell prawns and remove sand vein. In a large skillet, heat oil over medium high heat. Add shallots, garlic, and ginger and saute for a minute, stirring. Add prawns and lemon zest and cook until they turn pink. Deglaze pan with wine and remove prawns with a slotted spoon. Let wine reduce slightly, add reduced clam juice or stock, and swirl in butter. Return prawns to the pan and heat through. Meanwhile, cook fresh pasta in boiling salted water until al dente, about 2 to 3 minutes or about 8 minutes for dried pasta; drain. Add pasta to the skillet with prawns and sauce and mix lightly. Transfer to plates. Sprinkle with parsley and pistachios.

MAKES 4 SERVINGS.

Mocha Marron Coupe

Candied chestnuts, known by their French name marron glace, are a classic continental sweet savored during the Christmas season. Paired with a cognac and fudge sauce that sets into a chewy glaze, they make a peerless candy-like topping on an ice cream sundae.

4 ounces semisweet chocolate

¼ cup light corn syrup

¼ cup coffee

1 pint vanilla bean ice cream

*⅓ cup diced candied chestnuts
  and their syrup*

2 tablespoons cognac or rum (optional)

PLACE CHOCOLATE, CORN SYRUP, AND COFFEE IN THE TOP OF A DOUBLE BOILER. Heat over hot water, stirring, until chocolate melts and mixture is blended. Spoon ice cream into 4 large wine glasses or dessert bowls. Spoon over candied chestnuts and their syrup and drizzle over cognac or rum, if desired. Pour warm fudge sauce over ice cream. Serve at once.

MAKES 4 SERVINGS.

VARIATION: Prepare fudge sauce. Halve, core, and slice 4 Comice pears and arrange in four dessert bowls, points up. Scoop ice cream into 4 balls and nestle a ball in the center of each sliced pear. Spoon over fudge sauce and sprinkle with 3 tablespoons toasted chopped almonds.

Man has been eating chestnuts since prehistoric times. Roman legions are credited with having spread the chestnut and the walnut throughout Europe. Before the potato entered the French pantry, chestnuts were claimed to be the basic food of the poor. American Indians ground the nuts into flour for bread.

A Christmas Eve Fête

SHELLFISH PLATTER

BAGUETTES

CAESAR SALAD

CHRISTMAS COOKIES:
GINGERBREAD COOKIES, HEIRLOOM SUGAR COOKIES, SWEDISH SPRITZ,
TRIPLE NUT CHEWS, RASPBERRY FILBERT DROPS, SNOWBALLS

CHAMPAGNE, SPARKLING WINE, OR CHARDONNAY

WITH HOLIDAY ACTIVITIES OFTEN REACHING A CRESCENDO ON CHRISTMAS EVE, as last minute gifts are wrapped and tucked under the tree, a simple yet elegant supper is apropos. Shellfish is an excellent choice and a tradition in many lands. Crusty baguettes and a Caesar Salad round out the meal. For a wine accompaniment select Champagne, sparkling wine, or Chardonnay. Then pull out the cookie tins for a platterful of all the tempting favorites.

Shellfish Platter

This shellfish melange was a Portuguese discovery for me years ago at a wharfside cafe in Cascais. Portuguese cooks scoff at the notion of deveining shrimp and instead simmer them in their shells to imbue a richness to the broth. This creates a convivial dish that demands informality in the eating. Vary the shellfish selection depending on the availability in your region, as this is a flexible, accommodating dish. In the Northwest, the pink singing scallops are a natural. Mussels and prawns are usually available most anywhere.

2 dozen large prawns (about 1 pound)
2 dozen mussels, small rock clams, or singing scallops
3 lobster tails, washed and split
1½ cups dry white vermouth or dry white wine
¾ cup chopped Italian parsley or cilantro

3 cloves garlic, minced
¼ cup unsalted butter
Lemon wedges
Buttered baguette slices, lightly toasted

SCRUB THE SHELLFISH THOROUGHLY and place in a large soup kettle, along with the vermouth, ¼ cup of the parsley, and the garlic. Cover and simmer for 7 to 10 minutes or until the mussel or clam shells open. Transfer to a large platter and spoon the juices on top. Heat the butter and the remaining parsley until butter melts; spoon over the shellfish. Garnish with lemon wedges. Accompany with toasted baguette slices.

MAKES 6 SERVINGS.

Regional cooks might opt for Dungeness Crab Cioppino on the West Coast or Steamed Lobster in New England.

Caesar Salad

This beloved salad is credited to a Tijuana restaurateur named Caesar Cardini, who created it in the 1920s. The original version called for a coddled egg, but due to the salmonella risk, it is best omitted. This is a show-off salad that is often made at the table when dining out.

2 cloves garlic

½ cup olive oil

1 cup sourdough croutons

1 tablespoon balsamic vinegar

2 teaspoons Dijon mustard

2 tablespoons lemon juice

Salt and freshly ground black pepper to taste

2 inner heads of romaine

4 anchovy fillets, minced

⅓ cup grated Parmesan cheese

CRUSH GARLIC AND LET STEEP IN OIL 1 hour or longer for flavor to permeate. Toss croutons in 2 tablespoons of the oil, place in a baking pan, and bake in the middle of a preheated 325 degree oven for 10 to 12 minutes or until lightly toasted.

IN A SMALL BOWL, whisk together the remaining olive oil, garlic, vinegar, mustard, and lemon juice. Season with salt and pepper. Tear greens into bite-size pieces, dress and toss to coat. Mix in the anchovies. Sprinkle with croutons and cheese.

MAKES 6 SERVINGS.

NOTE: For a creamier dressing, place in a blender the 6 tablespoons oil, garlic, vinegar, and mustard. Whir for 10 seconds and blend in the lemon juice and anchovies. Season with salt and pepper.

Gingerbread Cookies

Baking dozens of gingerbread cookies and frosting each one artistically has been a yuletide tradition for four generations at a friend's California home. A well-worn brown paper bag spells out the ingredients and holds the cutters inside. Spicy aromas permeate the kitchen as counters are laden with baking sheets, each adorned with gaily decorated wreaths, red holly berries, trees with ornaments, whimsical Santas, and bells with silvery dragees.

Her mother-in-law launched the tradition when her six granddaughters were youngsters. She also started a custom of adding a doll collection to the tree each year. As she and her husband would travel in Europe, she would collect felt angels from Italy, wooden dolls from Germany, and china heads from Portugal. With an avid interest in lace, she crocheted stars for the tree and later for each of the girls' homes as they married.

The gingerbread recipe on its traveling bag always went to the ski house, and it still does. With lots of girls growing up, there were always lots of boys around and many had never baked cookies, let alone frosted them, so baking cookies became an indoor sport after a day on the slopes. They discovered how fun it was to bend the arms and legs of the cut-out dough so that the cookie people became lifelike in character.

Now with spouses and children in tow, the sisters all gather around my friend's expandable dining table to celebrate a joyful family Christmas, passing the cookies made weeks before and kept safely hidden in the freezer.

$\frac{1}{2}$ cup butter, at room temperature

$\frac{1}{2}$ cup sugar

1 egg

$\frac{1}{2}$ cup dark molasses

1 tablespoon cider vinegar

3 cups all-purpose flour

$\frac{3}{4}$ teaspoon baking soda

$\frac{1}{4}$ teaspoon salt

2 teaspoons ground ginger

$\frac{1}{2}$ teaspoon ground cinnamon

Frosting:

2 tablespoons butter

2 cups powdered sugar

1 teaspoon vanilla extract

3 to 4 tablespoons milk

Decorations: red cinnamon candies, green sugar, and silver dragees

IN A MIXING BOWL, CREAM BUTTER AND SUGAR UNTIL LIGHT IN COLOR. Mix in egg, molasses, and vinegar, beating until smooth. Stir together the flour, baking soda, salt, ginger, and cinnamon and mix in, beating just until blended. Chill 1 hour to firm up. On a lightly floured board, roll out the dough ⅛ inch thick and cut out with decorative cutters. Place on lightly greased baking sheets. Bake in the middle of a preheated 375 degree oven for 6 to 8 minutes or until golden brown on the edges. Let cool on a rack.

PREPARE THE FROSTING: In a small bowl, beat together butter, powdered sugar, vanilla, and enough milk to make a spreading consistency to the frosting. Frost decoratively.

MAKES ABOUT 8 DOZEN.

Queen Elizabeth is said to have invented gingerbread men by ordering that little cakes flavored with this spice be baked in the form of portraits of her familiars. The English carried their taste for ginger to America where it was included in the rations of American soldiers during the revolution. Ginger is originally native to tropical Asia. The misshapen flattened rhizomes were called hands or "races" in the spice trade.

Heirloom Sugar Cookies

This is a holiday favorite to cut into stars, bells, trees, angels, and other fanciful shapes. Before baking, sprinkle with sugar crystals.

1 cup butter, at room temperature

1¼ cups sugar

2 eggs

1 teaspoon vanilla extract

¼ teaspoon almond extract

3½ cups all-purpose flour

1 teaspoon baking powder

¼ teaspoon salt

Colored sugar sprinkles or coarse sugar crystals

IN A MIXING BOWL, BEAT BUTTER UNTIL CREAMY and beat in sugar, eggs, vanilla, and almond extract, beating until smooth. Stir together the flour, baking powder, and salt. Add to the creamed mixture; mixing until smooth. Cover and refrigerate 2 hours or longer to firm up. Take ¼ of the dough at a time and roll out on a lightly floured board to ⅛ inch thickness. Cut into desired shapes. Place on greased baking sheets. Sprinkle with colored sugar or crystals. Bake in the middle of a preheated 375 degree oven for 6 to 8 minutes or until lightly browned on the edges.

MAKES ABOUT 8 DOZEN.

Swedish Spritz

With our Swedish heritage, the buttery spritz was integral to our Christmas baking spree. As children we loved cranking the cookie press and cutting and twirling the dough into S's and O's. Mother often shaped the dough into wreaths jeweled with homemade raspberry jelly. A fast alternative is to squirt out the dough through the 1-inch-wide ridged cutter making long strips directly on the baking sheet. Bake until crispy and then cut diagonally.

1 cup butter, at room temperature

⅔ cup sugar

1 egg

1 teaspoon vanilla extract

½ teaspoon almond extract

2½ cups all-purpose flour

½ teaspoon baking powder

⅛ teaspoon salt

IN A MIXING BOWL, beat butter until creamy. Gradually add sugar and beat until light. Mix in egg, vanilla, and almond extract and beat until smooth. Stir together the flour, baking powder, and salt and add to the creamed mixture, mixing until smooth. Push dough through a crank-type cookie press using the thin flat wafer cut-out, making long strips on a lightly greased baking sheet. Bake in the middle of a preheated 350 degree oven for 8 minutes, or until the edges of the cookies are golden brown. Immediately cut diagonally across the strips with a knife making 1½ inch cookies. Transfer cookies to a rack to cool.

MAKES ABOUT 10 DOZEN.

NOTE: An aluminum crank-type cookie press is designed for spritz cookies is also useful as a basic decorating tube for icing cookies and cakes.

Triple Nut Chews

Recalling the cookies of my youth brings fond memories of a childhood brimming with filled cookie tins year around, yet special ones greeted the holiday season. Besides the ongoing baking at home, the neighborly doctor's wife delivered a plateful of sublime cookies each yuletide. My favorite among the dozens bestowed upon us were the chewy apricot nut drops. A caramel cookie barely bound together these chunky nut and fruit-laden morsels.

1½ cups Brazil nuts, coarsely chopped

1 cup filberts or almonds, coarsely chopped

½ cup walnuts or pecans, coarsely chopped

8 ounces (about 1¼ cups) whole pitted
   dates, coarsely chopped

1¼ cups dried apricots, coarsely chopped

¼ cup candied orange peel, finely chopped (optional)

1¼ cups all-purpose flour

½ teaspoon baking soda

½ teaspoon baking powder

1 teaspoon ground cinnamon

¼ teaspoon salt

½ cup butter, at room temperature

¾ cup firmly packed brown sugar

1 egg

IN A MEDIUM BOWL, mix nuts and fruits with ¼ cup of the flour and set aside. In another bowl, stir together remaining flour with baking soda, baking powder, cinnamon, and salt. In a mixing bowl, beat butter and brown sugar until light and creamy. Beat in egg. Add dry ingredients, mixing until smooth. Mix in fruit and nut mixture. Drop rounded teaspoons onto a greased baking sheet. Bake in the middle of a preheated 350 degree oven for 10 to 12 minutes, or until lightly browned. Let cool on wire racks.

MAKES ABOUT 4 DOZEN.

Raspberry Filbert Drops

These ambrosial cookies are tedious to produce but well worth the effort. Bake them with two kinds of jam for a colorful cookie plate.

½ cup butter, at room temperature
⅓ cup firmly packed brown sugar
1 egg, separated
½ teaspoon vanilla extract
1 cup all-purpose flour
⅛ teaspoon salt
⅔ cup finely chopped filberts or pecans
¼ cup raspberry or apricot jam

IN A MIXING BOWL, beat butter and sugar until creamy. Add egg yolk and vanilla and beat until smooth. Mix in flour and salt until dough clings together. Chill the dough for 30 minutes to firm up. Pinch off small balls of dough and roll between the palms of the hands to form ¾ inch balls. Flatten slightly. Whip egg white until frothy. With a fork dip each ball in slightly beaten egg white, then roll in chopped nuts to coat lightly. Place on a lightly greased baking sheet. With the tip of a finger, make a depression in the center of each cookie and fill with about ½ teaspoon of jam. Bake in the middle of a preheated 350 degree oven for 12 to 14 minutes or until lightly browned.

MAKES ABOUT 2½ DOZEN.

Snowballs

This timeless cookie can be found in many countries on holiday occasions. The names vary from Mexican Wedding Cakes, Viennese Pecan Crescents, to Greek Kourabiedes. The cookies are decorative shaped in crescents as well as rounds.

½ cup butter, at room temperature
¼ cup powdered sugar
1 teaspoon vanilla extract
1 cup all-purpose flour
⅛ teaspoon salt
1 cup finely chopped pecans, walnuts, almonds, or filberts
Powdered sugar for coating

IN A MIXING BOWL, beat butter and sugar until creamy. Add vanilla, flour, and salt and mix until smooth. Stir in nuts. Shape into ½-inch balls. Place on an ungreased baking sheet. Bake in the middle of a preheated 350 degree oven for 15 minutes or until lightly browned. Sift an ⅛-inch-thick layer of powdered sugar over a sheet of waxed paper. Transfer cookies to sugared paper. Sift more sugar over the top. Let cookies cool and store in an airtight container.

MAKES ABOUT 3 DOZEN.

Christmas Morning Brunch

FRESH FRUIT PLATTER

PANETTONE, GREEK CHRISTOPSOMO, AND RUSSIAN KRENDL

JARLSBERG OVEN OMELET

FRESHLY BREWED COFFEE

AROMATIC HOMEMADE BREAD IS INTEGRAL TO CHRISTMAS MORNING and every family has its favorite that draws on ethnic origins. A trio of golden breads offers a way to please many tastes and over the years in my home the choice encompasses these sweet loaves of Italian, Greek, and Russian heritage. It is smart to bake the breads in advance, then package and freeze them. To serve, let bread thaw, wrap in foil, and reheat in a 325 degree oven for 20 minutes on Christmas morning.

Augment the menu with a luscious platter of sliced fruit. Oranges, kiwi fruit, bananas, and seedless grapes or strawberries make a refreshing array. A hot oven omelet and steaming fresh ground coffee complete the brunch.

Panettone

For years my eye was attracted to the North Beach Italian bakeries in San Francisco that turned out tall loaves of panettone during the holiday season. Today this Milanese sweet bread has become generally available across America, pre-packaged in cylindrical paper wrappers and sold in gourmet shops or by mail order. Yet it's easy and so satisfying to produce a fruit-filled loaf at home. This one is superb, gilded with a crown of almond paste.

Sponge:

1 package active dry yeast

½ cup lukewarm water

½ cup unbleached flour

Pinch of sugar

Dough:

1 package active dry yeast

½ cup lukewarm water

1 cup golden raisins

2 tablespoons cognac or brandy

⅔ cup sugar

Grated zest of 2 oranges

Grated zest of 2 lemons

1 teaspoon vanilla extract

¼ teaspoon ground nutmeg

3 eggs

2 egg yolks

6 cups unbleached flour (approximately)

½ cup butter or margarine, at room temperature

1 cup milk, heated to lukewarm

1 teaspoon salt

½ cup slivered almonds

Almond Paste Topping: optional

½ cup blanched almonds

¼ cup sugar

2 egg whites

PREPARE THE SPONGE: In a small bowl, sprinkle yeast into the lukewarm water and stir in the flour and a pinch of sugar. Cover with plastic wrap and let stand in a warm place for 20 to 30 minutes or until bubbly and doubled in volume.

PREPARE THE DOUGH: In a large mixing bowl, sprinkle yeast into the lukewarm water and let stand until bubbly and doubled in volume, about 10 minutes. Place raisins in a microwave-safe bowl, add cognac, and let stand until plumped. To speed the process, microwave on high for 1 minute or bake in a preheated 300 degree oven for 10 minutes. Add the sponge to the dissolved yeast and beat thoroughly. Mix in the sugar, orange zest, lemon zest, vanilla, nutmeg, eggs, and egg yolks and beat well. Mix in 1 cup flour. Add butter, milk, salt, and 2 cups flour and mix thoroughly. Gradually add 2 more cups of flour and mix well using a heavy duty mixer or by hand. Then add enough remaining flour to make a soft dough. Mix in raisins and almonds. Turn out on a floured board and knead until smooth and elastic. Place in a bowl, cover with a towel, and let rise in a warm place until doubled in size, about 1½ hours.

TURN OUT ON A FLOURED BOARD AND KNEAD LIGHTLY. Divide in half. Shape into two round loaves and place in greased 2-quart souffle dishes or charlotte molds. Or divide into 5 pieces, shape in rounds, and place in 5 greased 1 pound coffee cans.

COVER WITH A TOWEL and let rise until doubled, about 45 minutes. (Dough should come just to the top of the coffee cans.)

(Continued next page)

MEANWHILE, PREPARE ALMOND PASTE TOPPING: In a food processor fitted with a steel blade, grind almonds finely. Add sugar and blend. Add egg whites and blend. Mixture will be runny. Spread almond paste on the top of the dough rounds. Place on a lower shelf in a preheated 400 degree oven; immediately turn temperature to 375 degrees and bake for 20 minutes. Reduce temperature to 350 degrees and bake 20 to 25 minutes longer for the large loaves or 10 to 15 minutes for the coffee can loaves. If tops brown too quickly cover with a sheet of foil. Let cool on racks for 10 minutes, then remove from pans. Makes 2 large loaves or five 1 pound loaves.

NOTE: The small coffee can loaves make charming gifts. Wrap in plastic wrap, place on a brown paper bag in a preheated 300 degree oven to "heat seal" for about a minute and the wrap will shrink.

Greek Christopsomo

Marrying into a Greek family in the fifties, I developed a love affair for the anise-scented Christopsomo, a 16-inch round yeast loaf that graced Yaya's table. It was a bread that she had grown up with in a little village in Greece, and she had continued the baking tradition when she moved to America. A symbolic cross, shaped of dough and jeweled with walnuts, tops this buttery Christmas bread. The slices are delicious served warm, unadorned, or toasted and spread with butter and honey.

The trick to serving this over-size bread with ease is to cut it lengthwise in thirds, then crosswise in slices.

4 teaspoons (about 1½ packages) active dry yeast

½ cup lukewarm water

5½ cups unbleached flour (approximately)

½ cup sugar

½ cup butter or margarine, at room temperature

4 eggs

1½ teaspoons salt

Zest of 2 oranges, cut into ¼ inch julienne strips

4 teaspoons anise seed

1 cup milk

9 walnut halves

PREPARE THE SPONGE: In a small bowl, sprinkle yeast over the lukewarm water and stir in ¾ cup of flour and 1 tablespoon of sugar; cover with plastic wrap, and let stand until bubbly and doubled in volume, about 30 minutes.

PREPARE THE DOUGH: In a large mixing bowl, beat butter and remaining sugar until creamy. Add eggs, salt, and orange zest and mix until blended. Add the sponge mixture and mix well. Crush anise seeds in a mortar with pestle. Heat milk and anise seeds until lukewarm and add to the mixture. Add 2 cups of flour and beat until smooth. Using a heavy duty mixer or by hand, gradually add remaining flour, adding just enough to make a soft dough. Mix with a dough hook for 10 minutes or turn out on a floured board and knead for 10 minutes. Place dough in a bowl, cover with a towel, and let rise in a warm place until doubled in size, about 1½ hours.

PUNCH DOWN, TURN OUT ON A FLOURED BOARD, and knead lightly to release air bubbles. Pinch off 2 balls of dough, each about 2½ inches in diameter, and set aside. Shape remaining ball of dough into a smooth flat cake about 9 inches in diameter, and place on a greased pizza pan or baking sheet. Roll each of the small balls into a 14-inch rope, and cut a 4-inch slash in the end of each. Cross ropes on the center of the round loaf. Curl each of the slashed sections away from center, forming two small circles at the end of each strip. Place a walnut half in each circle, and one in the center of the cross. Cover with a towel and set in a warm place until doubled in size, about 1 hour.

BAKE IN THE MIDDLE of a preheated 325 degree oven for 45 to 50 minutes or until golden brown and loaf sounds hollow when thumped. Be careful not to underbake. If necessary, cover with foil the last few minutes of baking to prevent overbrowning. Let cool on a rack.

MAKES 1 LARGE LOAF.

HINTS: When shaping the ropes of dough for the cross, stretch them out and let them rest a few minutes before continuing to stretch to the finished length. Then they will stretch with ease.
Use a vegetable peeler to peel off the orange zest into strips. Then cut crosswise into fine ribbons.

Russian Krendl

This pretzel-shaped bread is traditionally served as a holiday or birthday cake with candles encircling its curved sides. Cinnamon spices the tangy apricot and apple filling, encased in springy sweet bread.

1 package active dry yeast

¼ cup lukewarm water

½ cup milk

¼ cup butter or margarine

3 tablespoons sugar

1 teaspoon vanilla extract

½ teaspoon salt

3 egg yolks

2½ cups unbleached flour

Fruit Filling:

8 Granny Smith or Golden Delicious apples

1 tablespoon butter

4 tablespoons sugar

2 tablespoons lemon juice

⅓ cup chopped dried apricots

1 tablespoon melted butter

1 teaspoon ground cinnamon

Lemon Glaze:

1½ cups powdered sugar

2 tablespoons lemon juice

1 teaspoon grated lemon zest

Few drops water

IN A SMALL BOWL, sprinkle yeast into warm water and let stand until bubbly and doubled in volume, about 10 minutes. Heat milk and butter until lukewarm. Pour mixture into a mixing bowl. Stir in the sugar, vanilla, salt, egg yolks, and dissolved yeast. Beat until smooth. Gradually add flour, beating until smooth after each addition, and adding just enough flour to make a soft dough. Turn out onto a lightly floured board and knead until smooth. Place in a bowl and cover with a towel. Let rise in a warm place until doubled in size, about 1½ hours.

MEANWHILE PREPARE FRUIT FILLING: Peel, core, and thinly slice apples. In a large frying pan, heat butter, 2 tablespoons of the sugar, and lemon juice, add apples, and cook over medium high heat until apples are just tender, stirring and lifting to cook evenly. Add dried apricots.

TURN OUT DOUGH onto a floured board and knead lightly. Roll out into a rectangle about 9 inches wide and 28 inches long. Spread with melted butter. Mix remaining 2 tablespoons sugar with cinnamon and sprinkle over the butter. Spoon filling in a 3-inch strip down the center. Fold over 3 inches of the bottom lengthwise strip to cover the apples. Fold down the top lengthwise strip to cover it, making a strip about 3 inches wide and 28 inches long. Pinch the long ends to seal in the filling. Place on a greased baking sheet. Form into a stylized pretzel shape by bringing ends around in two half circles, touching at the center top, to make a dough pretzel about 9 x 16 inches. Then tuck ends under the center top of the roll. Cover with a towel and let rise in a warm place until doubled, about 45 minutes.

BAKE IN THE MIDDLE of a preheated 350 degree oven for 35 minutes or until golden brown. Let cool slightly.

PREPARE LEMON GLAZE (OPTIONAL): Mix together powdered sugar, lemon juice, and grated lemon zest and beat until smooth, adding a few drops water to make a spreading consistency.

Frost the cooled bread with Lemon Glaze.

MAKES 1 LOAF.

Jarlsberg Oven Omelet

This fast-to-assemble oven omelet is laced with melted cheese and ribbons of prosciutto.

8 eggs
1 cup milk
½ teaspoon salt
⅛ teaspoon white pepper
⅛ teaspoon ground nutmeg
2 ounces thinly sliced prosciutto or cooked ham, cut in strips
10 ounces (2½ cups) shredded Jarlsberg, Gruyere, or samsoe cheese
1 tablespoon butter, melted

IN A LARGE BOWL, beat eggs with a whisk until light and mix in milk, salt, pepper, nutmeg, prosciutto, and cheese. Pour into a buttered 2 quart baking dish about 10-½ inches in diameter. Drizzle top with melted butter. Bake in the middle of a preheated 350 degree oven for 30 to 35 minutes or until set, and lightly browned.

MAKES 6 TO 8 SERVINGS.

A Festive Christmas Dinner

SMOKED SALMON CORNUCOPIAS WITH BUTTERED PUMPERNICKEL

ROAST PRIME RIB OF BEEF WITH YORKSHIRE PUDDING AND HORSERADISH SAUCE

TWICE-BAKED STUFFED POTATOES

MUSHROOMS IN HERB CREAM   BROCCOLI FLOWERETS

SPINACH SALAD WITH TOASTED PINE NUTS

STEAMED PERSIMMON PUDDING

CHOCOLATE YULE LOG

CHARDONNAY   CABERNET SAUVIGNON

THIS FESTIVE HOLIDAY DINNER RELIES ON TIMELESS FAVORITES. Smoked salmon partnered with buttered pumpernickel makes a stylish first course with Chardonnay. The cornerstone of the meal is a standing rib roast, a classic English favorite to deck out with Yorkshire Pudding and zesty fresh horseradish sauce. Accompaniments include twice-baked potato boats, mushrooms sealed in herb sauce, steamed broccoli flowerets, and a spinach salad. An aged Cabernet Sauvignon is a choice companion for the main course. The dessert finale features two charmers: a steamed pudding and a chocolate whipped cream roll.

Roast Prime Rib of Beef with Yorkshire Pudding

A stately standing rib roast is is one of the easiest entrees to prepare. Allow about 1 pound of meat per person because of the bone and figure on roasting 15 minutes per pound if over 5 pounds or 20 minutes per pound if under 5 pounds. Timing will vary with the shape of the roast so a meat thermometer is a necessity.

1 3 or 4 rib beef roast
Salt and freshly ground pepper

Yorkshire Pudding:
2 tablespoons drippings from roasting pan
2 eggs
1 cup milk
1 cup all-purpose flour
½ teaspoon salt

Horseradish Sauce:
½ cup grated horseradish root
1 cup sour cream
Salt and freshly ground pepper to taste

INSERT A MEAT THERMOMETER IN THE ROAST and place fat side up on a rack in a shallow open pan. Roast in the lower part of a preheated 325 degree oven for about 15 minutes per pound or until a meat thermometer registers 130 degrees for rare or 140 degrees for medium rare. Transfer to a board and let rest. Pour pan drippings into a 9 inch square pan. Place in a preheated 425 degree oven and heat through. In a mixing bowl, beat eggs until blended and mix in milk, flour, and salt, beating until smooth. Pour batter into the hot pan and bake in a 425 degree oven for 25 to 30 minutes or until puffed and golden brown.

PREPARE HORSERADISH SAUCE: In a bowl, mix together the grated horseradish, sour cream, and salt and pepper to taste. Refrigerate until serving time.

Carve roast and serve pudding alongside the roast. Pass Horseradish Sauce.

MAKES ABOUT 8 SERVINGS.

This old-fashioned pudding was often baked right in the drippings in the roasting pan and served as a course preceding the roast.

Twice-Baked Stuffed Potatoes

Buttery mashed potatoes piled inside their crispy skins are the ultimate comfort food — neat "boats" with the regal roast.

8 medium-large baking potatoes
4 tablespoons butter
1 cup hot milk or light cream (approximately)
Salt to taste
2 tablespoons chopped chives (optional)

WASH AND SCRUB EVEN-SIZED, SHAPELY POTATOES. Dry and grease them lightly with butter. Bake in the middle of a preheated 425 degree oven for 25 minutes. Pull out the rack and quickly puncture the skin once with a fork, permitting steam to escape. Return to oven and finish baking, about 15 minutes to 25 minutes longer.

REMOVE FROM OVEN and let cool for a few minutes. Slice off a lid about ¼ way down, horizontally on the potatoes. Set aside. Scoop out the insides of the potatoes being careful to leave the skin intact and place into a mixing bowl. Add butter, milk, and salt. Mash and whip potatoes until smooth. If necessary, add more milk to whip to desired consistency. Pile into the potato shells. Place in a baking pan and return to a 425 degree oven to brown lightly, about 15 minutes. Sprinkle with chives.

MAKES 8 SERVINGS.

Mushrooms in Herb Cream

Herbs and cream gild these mushrooms for a flavor-packed side dish.

3 tablespoons butter

1 tablespoon olive oil

1½ pounds small button mushrooms, sliced

2 shallots, finely chopped

Salt and freshly ground pepper to taste

¾ cup sour cream

¼ cup minced parsley

2 tablespoons minced chives

¾ teaspoon crumbled dried tarragon

Chopped parsley and chives for garnish

IN A LARGE FRYING PAN, heat butter and oil over medium high heat. Add mushrooms and shallots and sauté for 5 to 6 minutes, stirring or shaking pan, until mushrooms just begin to brown slightly. Season with salt and pepper to taste. Remove from heat and stir in sour cream, parsley, chives, and tarragon. Heat through, but do not boil. Garnish with chopped parsley and chives.

MAKES 8 SERVINGS.

Spinach Salad with Toasted Pine Nuts

This fresh tasting salad flaunts a holiday color scheme.

Vinaigrette:
½ cup olive oil
3 tablespoons red wine vinegar
1 clove garlic, minced
Salt and freshly ground pepper to taste
2 teaspoons Dijon mustard
2 shallots, chopped

2 cups cherry tomatoes, halved if large
2 bunches spinach, trimmed
4 ounces alfalfa sprouts
⅓ cup toasted pine nuts or roasted sunflower seeds

PREPARE VINAIGRETTE: Mix together in a small bowl the oil, vinegar, garlic, salt, pepper, mustard, and shallots. Add cherry tomatoes and let stand for 1 hour. Tear spinach into bite-size pieces and place in a bowl. Add sprouts. Pour dressing over the greens and tomatoes. Toss lightly. Sprinkle with nuts or seeds.

MAKES 8 SERVINGS.

Steamed Persimmon Pudding

With bright orange persimmons hanging heavy on garden trees, California cooks have geared the holiday pudding to this fruit to create a delectable dark and spicy torte, lighter than the classic English plum pudding.

*1 cup puréed persimmons (about 2 large
  persimmons with skins removed)*

2 teaspoons baking soda

½ cup butter, at room temperature

1¼ cups firmly packed brown sugar

2 eggs

2 tablespoons cognac or rum

1 cup whole-wheat flour

1 teaspoon ground cinnamon

¼ teaspoon ground nutmeg

½ teaspoon salt

¾ cup chopped walnuts or almonds

¾ cup golden raisins

Vanilla ice cream

FILL A LARGE PAN with enough water to come halfway up the sides of a 2 quart pudding mold. Bring to a boil over medium heat. Place persimmon purée in a bowl and stir in the baking soda; the mixture will thicken. In a mixing bowl, cream butter and sugar until light. Add eggs and cognac and beat well. Stir together the flour, cinnamon, nutmeg, and salt and mix in. Add persimmon mixture and mix until blended. Stir in nuts and raisins. Transfer into a greased and floured 2 quart mold. Cover tightly with a lid or foil. Place on a rack in the pot so simmering water covers pan sides halfway. Let steam for 2 hours. Remove from the pan and let rest 10 minutes. Turn out onto a rack. Serve while still warm, or reheat in a 325 degree oven for 10 to 15 minutes. Cut in slices and top with a scoop of vanilla ice cream.

MAKES 8 SERVINGS.

NOTE: Two one-pound coffee cans make good containers instead of a 2-quart mold.

Chocolate Yule Log

The ultimate dessert of a French Christmas day feast is the Buche de Noel, *a yule log cake adorned with whimsical meringue or marzipan mushrooms. Often it is a golden cake with chocolate butter cream swirled inside. This souffle-like chocolate roll variation produces a sumptuous cake pinwheeled with whipped cream. Light and ethereal, it is surprisingly fast to make. Mother would turn out this childhood favorite of mine in seconds with the commercial Hobart mixer.*

¼ cup unsweetened European-style
  cocoa

1 cup plus 2 tablespoons unsifted
  powdered sugar

1 tablespoon all-purpose flour

6 eggs, separated

⅛ teaspoon salt

⅛ teaspoon cream of tartar

2 teaspoons vanilla extract

Powdered sugar

1 cup whipping cream

SIFT TOGETHER OR PUSH THROUGH A SIEVE into a bowl the cocoa, 1 cup sugar, and flour. Beat the egg whites until foamy, add salt and cream of tartar, and beat until soft peaks form. Then beat in the remaining 2 tablespoons of powdered sugar. Set aside. Beat egg yolks until thick and lemon colored, add 1 teaspoon of the vanilla, and mix in the dry ingredients. Then gently fold in the egg white meringue. Grease a 10 by 15 inch baking pan, line it with waxed paper, and butter and flour the paper. Spread batter evenly in pan and bake in the middle of a preheated 400 degree oven for 10 minutes, or until the top springs back when touched lightly. Immediately turn out on a towel dusted with powdered sugar and peel off waxed paper. Roll up from a narrow end, rolling the towel up inside, and let cool.

Whip cream until soft peaks form and flavor with 1 tablespoon powdered sugar and 1 teaspoon vanilla. Unroll cake, spread cream filling over it, and roll up again. Transfer to a serving plate and chill until ready to serve, or up to 6 hours. Just before serving sift powdered sugar over the cake. Slice slightly on the diagonal to serve.

MAKES 6 TO 8 SERVINGS.

NOTE: If desired for an adult dessert, flavor the whipped cream with 2 tablespoons Cointreau, Amaretto, or rum and omit vanilla.

Food Gifts

A GIFT FROM THE KITCHEN IS A HEART-WARMING TREAT FOR A SPECIAL FRIEND OR NEIGHBOR. It is fun to prepare the specialty of the house — a culinary condiment or sweet — in quantity and then package it in a festive way, wrapped in see-through cellophane and beribboned or tucked in a fancy tin.

There are countless possibilities: pesto, spiced nuts, herb-flavored vinegar and oils, dried plum tomatoes or apricots, and holiday cookies or tea breads. Special chutneys and jams made in the summertime are apropos. Let whatever is abundant in the garden or pantry provide inspiration.

One year in a tempo of ambition in my kitchen, three dozen Italian bread doves sealed with almond paste were baked, shrunk-wrapped, and delivered to friends, while our two-year-old had great fun prying open the 4 pound can of almond paste and scooping out a mouthful.

This season, chocolate-tipped candied orange peel triangles, an almond crunch toffee, and garlic and rosemary vinegar made with garden bounty make excellent treats.

Chocolate-Dipped Candied Orange Peel

For gift giving, wrap small bundles of candied peel in clear cellophane and tie with a bow for a pretty package.

Peel of 4 oranges, cut into quarters

Water

1⅓ cups sugar

6 ounces semisweet chocolate

PLACE QUARTERED ORANGE PEEL IN A SAUCEPAN. Cover with water and bring to a boil. Simmer for 1 minute, then pour off water. Cover again with water and bring to a boil. Simmer for 1 minute; pour off water. Combine sugar and 1⅓ cups water in a saucepan. Bring to a boil. Scrape off most of the white pith from the orange peel. Cut peel into triangles, about 1 inch long and ½ inch across at the base. Add orange triangles to the syrup and let cook, uncovered, until the syrup is totally absorbed. Transfer to waxed paper and let dry. If still moist, sprinkle lightly with sugar. Meanwhile, melt chocolate in a double boiler over hot water. Dip the tips of orange triangles in chocolate, coating half of them. Lay on foil and let cool. When firm, store in an airtight container.

MAKES ABOUT 6 DOZEN.

Almond Toffee

It is smart to package this candy in small decorative tins to keep it fresh and crispy.

½ pound butter

1¼ cups sugar

½ teaspoon baking soda

1 package (6 ounces) semisweet chocolate chips

⅓ cup finely chopped toasted almonds

COMBINE BUTTER AND SUGAR IN A SAUCEPAN and heat over medium-high heat, stirring, until mixture comes to a boil. Cover and simmer for 3 minutes. Uncover and continue cooking until temperature reaches 290 degrees on a candy thermometer, stirring occasionally. Remove from heat; immediately add baking soda, stirring it in quickly, and pour out onto a 10 by 15-inch baking pan lined with buttered foil. Sprinkle chocolate chips over the top and let cool for a few minutes. The chocolate will melt from the heat of the toffee. Spread chocolate with a spatula to make a smooth coating, then sprinkle with nuts. Let cool until set. Then peel off the foil and break candy into chunks. Store in an airtight container.

MAKES ABOUT 3 DOZEN PIECES OF TOFFEE.

Garlic and Rosemary Vinegar

Slender bottles with a screw cap or cork are suitable for holding this herb vinegar.

2 cups red wine vinegar
2 cups white wine or white distilled vinegar

8 cloves garlic, peeled
4 5-inch sprigs rosemary

COMBINE VINEGARS IN A SAUCEPAN and heat until simmering. Spear garlic at each end of a rosemary sprig and place in a large jar. Pour hot vinegar into the jar, let cool, and cap jar. Let sit for 1 week, turning jar occasionally. Decant into 8-ounce bottles, placing a garlic-tipped rosemary sprig in each. Tightly cap or cork bottles and store in a cool, dark place.

MAKES 4 8-OUNCE BOTTLES

Index of Recipes

Almond Toffee   70

Angel Hair Pasta with Ginger Prawns   35

Black Bean Soup   26

Caesar Salad   41

Caramelized Sweet Onions   18

Chocolate Almond Torte   29

Chocolate-Dipped Candied Orange Peel   76

Chocolate Yule Log   67

Cinnamon Crisp Apple Pie   23

Cranberry Apple Relish   16

Garlic and Rosemary Vinegar   71

Gingerbread Cookies   43

Glazed Carrots   17

Greek Christopsomo   55

Green Beans With Herbs   19

Green Salad with Avocado, Pink Grapefruit, and
   Pomegranate Seeds   13

Heirloom Sugar Cookies   45

Jarlsberg Oven Omelet   59

Mocha Marron Coupe   36

Mulled Wine   31

Mushrooms in Herb Cream   64

Panettone   52

Praline Pecan Pumpkin Pie   20

Roast Prime Rib of Beef with Yorkshire Pudding   62

Raspberry Filbert Drops   48

Roast Turkey with Sage Stuffing   14

Roasted Yams   17

Russian Krendl   57

Shellfish Platter   40

Snowballs   49

Southwest Salad   28

Spinach Salad with Toasted Pine Nuts   65

Steamed Persimmon Pudding   66

Swedish Spritz   46

Toasted Walnut, Endive, and Apple Salad   34

Triple Nut Chews   47

Twice-Baked Stuffed Potatoes   63